P9-EMG-486

Other Books by Richard N. Bolles

The Three Boxes of Life,
   and How to Get Out of Them

What Color Is Your Parachute?

Where Do I Go From Here With My Life?
   (co-authored with John C. Crystal)

The New Quick
Job-Hunting Map

Richard Nelson Bolles
author of
What Color Is Your Parachute?

1๑ Ten Speed Press

P O Box 7123   Berkeley, California 94707

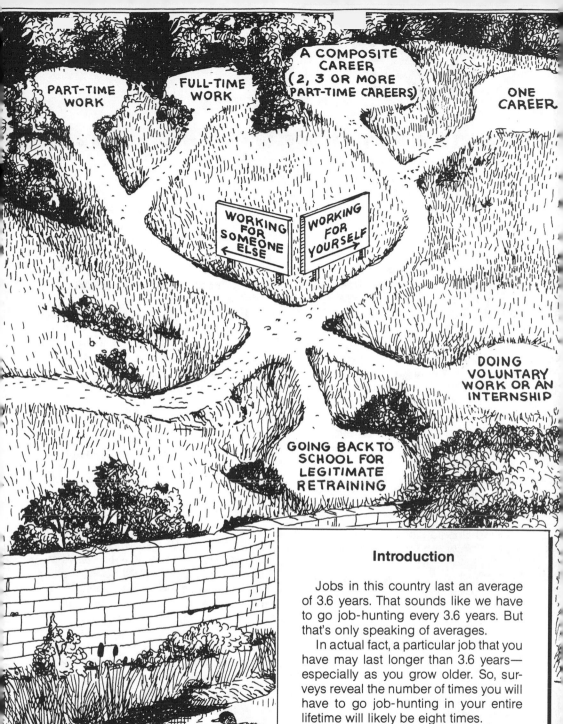

PART-TIME
WORK

FULL-TIME
WORK

A COMPOSITE
CAREER
(2, 3 OR MORE
PART-TIME CAREERS)

ONE
CAREER

WORKING
FOR
SOMEONE
ELSE

WORKING
FOR
YOURSELF

DOING
VOLUNTARY
WORK OR AN
INTERNSHIP

GOING BACK TO
SCHOOL FOR
LEGITIMATE
RETRAINING

Introduction

Jobs in this country last an average of 3.6 years. That sounds like we have to go job-hunting every 3.6 years. But that's only speaking of averages.

In actual fact, a particular job that you have may last longer than 3.6 years—especially as you grow older. So, surveys reveal the number of times you will have to go job-hunting in your entire lifetime will likely be eight times.

When it is time for you to go job-hunting, there are many roads you can take. They are shown on the map above.

TO PUT THE MAP INTO WORDS

These are the choices facing You:

(1) □ Should I make a career change? OR
　　□ Should I stay in the same field/career?

(2) If I choose to stay in the same field/career:
　　□ Should I move to a different organization, though staying in the same type of job? OR
　　□ Should I stay in the same organization where I am now?

(3) If the same organization:
　　□ Should I stay in the very same job as I am now in? OR
　　□ Should I move to a different department or different job there?

(4) If I make a career change:
　　□ Should I change careers by going back to school for retraining? OR
　　□ Should I change careers without going back to school?

(5) If I change careers without further schooling:
　　□ Should I look for a new career in which I work for someone else? OR
　　□ Should I look for a new career in which I work for myself?

(6) If I look for a new career in which I work for someone else:
　　□ Should I seek a job at decent or even high pay? OR
　　□ Should I seek for a volunteer job at first, or even an internship?

(7) If I look for a new career in which I work for myself:
　　□ Should I seek a career made up of just one job? OR
　　□ Should I seek a composite career, made up of several (2-5) different jobs/careers?

(8) And, once I have answered all the above questions, *what* is it I should do?

You need to work your way through these decisions. It may at first sight seem to you that each pair of decisions requires a different pathway. This is not true.

They are all approached by the same pathway—a basic "trunk" road that precedes them all.

This "trunk" road has three sections to it, and you MUST travel all three sections—no matter which road through Job Land you are currently leaning toward. The three sections you MUST cover, are:

1. **WHAT.** This has to do with your skills. You need to inventory and identify what skills you have that you most enjoy using. These are called transferable skills, because they are transferable to any field/career that you choose, regardless of where you first picked them up.

2. **WHERE.** This has to do with jobs as environments. Think of yourself as a flower. You know that a flower which blooms in the desert will not do well at 10,000 feet up—and vice versa. Every flower has an environment where it does best. So with you. You are like a flower. You need to decide where you want to use your skills, where you would thrive, and do your most effective work.

3. **HOW.** You need to decide how to get where you want to go. This has to do with finding out the names of the jobs you would be most interested in, AND the names of organizations (in your preferred geographical area) which have such jobs to offer, AND the names of the people or person there who actually has the power to hire you.

And, how you can best approach that person to show him or her how your skills can help them with their problems. How, if you were hired there, you would not be part of the problem, but part of the solution.

Now, to be sure, these three basic sections of your job-hunting or career-changing road will be traveled in a slightly different way, depending on your goals. If you ultimately become sure that you want to go into business for yourself, then the HOW will consist in identifying all the people who have already done something like the thing you are thinking of, so that you can go interview them and profit from their learnings and mistakes before you set out on your own. And the HOW may consist in identifying the potential customers or clients who would use your services or buy your product.

But, adaptation aside, you WILL need to travel all three sections of this basic trunk road, regardless of where you plan to end up. The only exception to this rule, is if you plan on staying at the same job and in the same organization where you presently are; and you are using this Map only to get a better picture of your strengths. In this case, you will omit the HOW picture—but will still need to travel the WHAT and WHERE sections of the road. For even if you plan on remaining where you are—as it is already the "ideal" job for you—you will still function much better there if you know more intimately what your skills or strengths are, and where you like to use them.

(As one satisfied worker put it, "The skills inventory is something I do every two or three years. Each time I do it, I find out more specific things about what I do well. This information tells me what to watch for in the world—what kind of tasks I can volunteer for and do very well at. I know more about the *kind* of thing I want to be, do, be surrounded by. I am now sensitized and ready to recognize them when they swim by.")

THE RULE:
TAKE NO SHORTCUTS

Aside from this special case of staying right where you are, you WILL need to travel all three sections of the road, WHAT, WHERE and HOW.

If you only do the homework on the WHAT, you will be like a cart without any horse to pull it. It just stands helplessly beside the road.

"WHAT" furnishes you with the cart; "WHERE" furnishes the horse to pull it; and "HOW" furnishes the road along which your cart and horse travel, to your chosen destination.

Handicaps

Most of us think that when we go job-hunting, we need a special road, just for us. You probably think you have some special handicap in the job-hunt, that requires special handling. Here is a list of some of these handicaps—an expansion of a list originally put together by Daniel Porot, the job-hunting expert of Europe.

You may check off the ones which apply to you:

☐ I am just graduating
☐ I just graduated
☐ I graduated too long ago
☐ I am a woman
☐ I am a self-made man
☐ I am too young
☐ I am too old
☐ I have a prison record
☐ I have a psychiatric history
☐ I have never held a job before
☐ I have only had one employer
☐ I am a foreigner
☐ I have not had enough education
☐ I have had too much education
☐ I am too much of a generalist
☐ I am too much of a specialist
☐ I am a clergyperson
☐ I am Hispanic
☐ I am Black
☐ I am just coming out of the military
☐ I have a physical handicap
☐ I have a mental handicap
☐ I have only worked for large employers
☐ I have only worked for small employers
☐ I am too shy
☐ I am too assertive
☐ I come from a very different kind of background
☐ I come from another industry
☐ I come from another planet

If you checked off any of these, this makes you a handicapped job-hunter or career-changer. Most of us are so handicapped. The true meaning of the above comprehensive list is that there are about three weeks of your life when you're employable. That is, if handicaps cannot be overcome.

But of course they can be overcome. There are, after all, two kinds of employers (or clients or customers) out there:

those who will be put off by your handicap, and therefore won't hire you; AND

those who are NOT put off by your handicap, and therefore will hire you if you are qualified for the job.

You are not interested in the former kind of employer, client or customer. No matter how many of them there are. You are only looking for those employers who are NOT put off by your handicap, and therefore will hire you if you are qualified for the job.

As Tom Jackson, author of *Guerilla Tactics in the Job Market,* has well observed, the job-hunting process may best be described as NO NO NO NO NO NO NO NO NO NO NO NO NO NO NO NO NO NO NO NO NO NO NO NO NO NO NO NO NO NO NO NO NO NO NO NO NO NO NO NO NO NO NO NO NO NO NO NO NO NO NO NO NO NO NO NO NO NO NO NO NO NO NO NO NO NO NO NO NO NO NO NO NO NO NO NO NO NO NO NO NO NO NO NO YES.

It only takes one YES from the organization you wish most to work for, to get you the job. Every "No" that you get out of the way, as you go, will bring you that much closer to the only YES you need to hear.

The most important thing for you to know is that your best chance of bridging whatever handicap you have or think you have is CAREFUL PREPARATION ON YOUR PART.

The employers, clients, customers who will not care about your handicap will be most impressed if you approach them, not as a job-beggar, but as a resource person. Preparation such as this Map will change you from a job-beggar into A Resource Person.

In this sense, the trunk road, about which we have been talking,—the WHAT, WHERE, and HOW—is a bridge over whatever handicap you may have.

What It Takes
To Find A Job

What will it take for you to successfully get over that bridge? What will it take for you to do the WHAT, WHERE and HOW most effectively?

You want, of course, to hear that the answer is a bunch of sure-fire techniques, which we are about to teach you in this Map.

Alas, there are no techniques which will *guarantee* that you will find a job, if only you follow them faithfully.

Any true job-hunting veteran will tell you in all honesty that it takes three things to find a job:

a. Techniques. There are things others can teach you, and they will increase your effectiveness and improve your chances. You need to take these very seriously. But, by themselves, these are not enough.

b. Art. As in the phrase: "There's a real art to the way she does that." We refer here to the special stamp that each person's individuality puts on what they do. A certain amount of the job-hunt others cannot teach you. You bring your own unique art to the job-hunt, as you do to everything else you do. It's that extra pizazz, enthusiasm, energy that is uniquely yours, which must be present, before you can be successful at the job-hunt. We cannot clone you. Genuine individuality always marks every successful job-hunt.

c. Luck. Following certain techniques faithfully, and combining them with your own individual art in the way you do it, will not in and of themselves get you the job. There is always a certain amount of luck involved in any successful job-hunt. You have to be the right person in the right place at the right time.

These factors have varying importance, depending on which part of the job-hunt you are dealing with.

Your own individual way of doing things, your "art," is most important during the WHAT. This is because skill identification is more of an art, than a science. We can give you the basic rules, but a lot of it you have to do in your own individual way.

Techniques become more important during the WHERE and the HOW: those parts of the job-hunt can more easily be defined.

And Luck becomes most important during the HOW part of your job-hunt. So, if you like diagrams, your job-hunt will come out looking something like this:

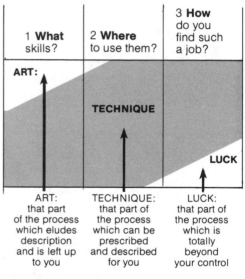

What Can This Map Give You?
Obviously, this Map cannot give you good luck, or give you individuality. You must already possess that individuality, and you must have lady luck smile on you, for your job-hunt to succeed. BUT, by using the techniques in this Map and in the accompanying text book, *What Color Is Your Parachute?*, the amount of luck you will need is greatly reduced. "Luck favors the prepared mind," as someone has observed. This Map, if followed faithfully, WILL give you a thoroughly prepared mind.

Now, on to the details of the trunk road to Job Land, the bridge over handicaps: WHAT, WHERE and HOW.

What

What Skills You Have and Most Enjoy Using

The easiest way to get into the subject of your skills is to just dive in. Imagine, if you will, that this diagram below is the aerial view of a room in which a Party is taking place (the view is taken from the next floor up). At this Party, for some unknown reason, people with similar interests or skills have gathered together with one another, in the same corner of the room. As there are basically six such groups, it is fortunate the room has six corners:

1

People who have athletic or mechanical ability, prefer to work with objects, machines, tools, plants, or animals, or to be outdoors

2

People who like to observe, learn, investigate, analyze, evaluate, or solve problems

6

People who like to work with data, have clerical or numerical ability, carrying things out in detail or following through on other's instructions

The Party

People who have artistic, innovating or intuitional abilities, and like to work in unstructured situations, using their imagination or creativity

3

People who like to work with people — influencing, persuading or performing or leading or managing for organizational goals or for economic gain

People who like to work with people — to inform, enlighten, help, train, develop, or cure them, or are skilled with words

5

4

It is a party that is to go on, all through the night. You are told that you must choose to be with one of the groups in one of the corners of the room.

a) Which corner of the room would you instinctively be drawn to, as "your kind of people"—whom you would most *enjoy* being with, for the longest time? Leave aside any question of shyness; maybe they will do all the talking, and you can just listen, with rapt attention. Write the *number* for that corner here:

b) Suppose for some reason *that* group left the party, without you. (They have gone to another party, crosstown. How inconsiderate!) Of the groups which *still remain* at *this* Party, which group would you *now* be most drawn to, as "your kind of people"? Write the *number* for their corner here:

c) For some reason, this group also leaves for another party crosstown. (Hey, get the address of *that* party.) Of the groups which now remain, which one would you enjoy being with the most, and for the longest time? Write the *number* of that corner here:

Incidentally, if you don't like the metaphor of a Party, think of this as a bookstore, with different book sections; or a job fair, with different employers ready to talk to you, or whatever. The issue is: which group of people, subjects, interests, or skills, are you most attracted to?

You can go back now, if you wish, and underline specific skills within each of your favorite three groups, that are the skills you like the very best.

There, you have done what we call "elementary skill identification"—and in less than three minutes. This was just to give you a quick "feel" for the exercise. The principle on which this exercise was based, is that *we are instinctively attracted to people who are doing what we would like to do. And we would like to do those things which we already do well, and enjoy.*

That's all.

Now that you've taken your first step on the bridge of WHAT skills you have and most enjoy using, let's really roll up our sleeves, and get to work.

You Are Going To Go On A 'Verb Hunt'

The skills you are now going to go hunting for, are called "transferable skills" or "functional skills." In order to find them, it is going to be necessary for you to write out some simple statements about something you did in the past.

Here is a simple example: "(I) *organized* a committee in our community, which raised $15,000 to help a family that had been burnt out of their home on Christmas Eve."

Hidden in that statement, and all such statements about your past, is a key *skill* word. It is always a verb, or a noun made out of a verb. In this particular example, it is the word "organized." That is a skill. We can of course later put the skill in various forms: *organized,* effectively *organizes,* able *to organize,* good at *organizing,* or adept at *organization.*

We can play around with the tense and form of it, later. But for now, as you write out your statements, the verb will be in the past tense, such as "organized." The skill is in the verb. And it is convincing. For, clearly you possess the

skill, since you have already demonstrated you do.

Notice that in the above example the word "I" is in parentheses. It's fine where it is, in this statement about the past. But when it comes time for you to polish and shine your skill identifications later, you will then want to wipe out the "I." It is normally *omitted* in any final definition of your skill, such as a letter or resume or 'qualifications brief.' You will be listing a number of skills at that time, and the word "I" in front of each one is totally unnecessary. After all, if it's your statement, we know who did it. You won't need to keep telling us "I."

In skill identification, first and last, it is not the noun but the *verb* that is important. That is why you may think of this part of your job-hunt—the WHAT phase —as essentially "a verb hunt."

You Need Some Stories— Seven, To Be Exact

We can't just go hunting for *verbs* by themselves. Though, you can always try that approach. You will almost certainly discover, however, that the verbs are best found in stories. So, you need to write out some stories about your past. Ultimately, you are going to need seven such stories. These stories need to be:

1. *Brief.* A paragraph or two, at most.

2. *Experiences in which You are the chief actor or actress.* Telling us a story about something done *to* you, like being given an award or something, will NOT do. It must be something YOU did. Then it's all right if there's an award, at the end.

3. *Experiences in which You accomplished something.* There must have been:

a. Some kind of problem you needed to solve.

b. Some kind of action that you took, in order to solve it.

c. Some concrete results that could be seen, or even better, measured.

4. *Experiences in which you were truly enjoying yourself.* You can dredge up Skills from anything you have ever done, anyplace. *But* what you are looking for are the Skills you used *when you were enjoying yourself, accomplishing something.*

5. *Taken from any period of your life, and from any part of your life: work OR leisure OR learning.*

6. *Told step-by-step, in detail.*

You Need Seven Sheets Of Paper

For this exercise, you will eventually need seven blank sheets of notebook paper: one sheet for each story/job/role.

But, you start out with just one sheet, for you begin by writing just one story.

Do that NOW, please.

THIS WON'T DO

THIS WILL DO

SAMPLE

"The Halloween Experience.
I won a prize on Halloween
for dressing up as a
horse."

SAMPLE

"My Halloween Experience When
I Was Seven Years Old. Details:

When I was seven, I decided I wanted
to go out on Halloween dressed as a
horse. I wanted to be the front end of
the horse, and I talked a friend of mine
into being the back end of the horse.
But, at the last moment he backed out,
and I was faced with the prospect of
not being able to go out on Halloween.
At this point, I decided to figure out
some way of getting dressed up as the
whole horse, myself. I took a fruit
basket, and tied some string to both
sides of the basket's rim, so that I could
tie the basket around my rear end. This
filled me out enough so that the
costume fit me, by myself. I then fixed
some strong thread to the tail so that
I could make it wag by moving my
hands. When Halloween came I not
only went out and had a ball,
but I won a prize as well."

If you *absolutely* can't think of any experiences you've had where you enjoyed yourself, and accomplished something, then try this: Describe the seven most enjoyable *jobs* that you've had; or seven *roles* you've had so far in your life, such as: wife, mother, cook, homemaker, volunteer in the community, citizen, dressmaker, student, etc. Tell us something you did or accomplished, in each role.

Let us stop equating work with earning a living, but rather think of it as an important component of making a life.

—Ralph C. Weinrich, *Michigan Business Review*

You Need A List (Of Skills)

Once you have the story written, you will want to go back over it and identify the skills that you used in that story (in the doing of it, not the telling of it). Here we run into a problem. Not every verb is a skill. And sometimes the verb you want, is only implied in the story.

So, what are you do to? Try to name the skills, off the top of your head? Most of us have poor luck when we try to do this. We know what we did, but we run out of words to describe it. Therefore, sooner or later—usually sooner—we cry out for a list. We need a list. That's what this Map is here to give you.

You Need People, Or Data Or Things

How many skill verbs should be on the list? Well, the answer could be "thousands." After all, there are at least 12,000 different jobs in this world. There are 8,000 alternate titles for those 12,000 jobs. So, there are at least 20,000 different job titles you can choose from; and heaven only knows how many skills lie beneath those titles. *Too* many! We need some way to simplify the list. *Fortunately,* there is such a way.

All jobs deal with three things. And only three. So, ultimately all transferable skills deal with only three things, too.

Your skills are either:

skills with **People**, or

skills with **Information**,
   sometimes called **Data**, or

skills with **Things**.

You have all three, in varying degrees. The question is, what are the particular skills that you have with each? *And,* which of these do you enjoy the most? That is what you now need to explore.

Basically there are only 13 things you can do with People (plus one additional group, for work with animals). And there are only 15 things you can do with Information, or Data. And there are only 11 things you can do with Things. Every other skill identification is a variation, or a sub-particle of these 40:

If you want some definitions of PEOPLE, INFORMATION/DATA, and THINGS, here goes:

• PEOPLE may mean all kinds of people, or very specific kinds of people—defined by age, culture, background, kinds of problems they face, etc. PEOPLE also includes animals, and beings from other orders of Reality.

• INFORMATION/DATA may mean information, knowledge, data, ideas, facts, figures, statistics, etc. Information is present in every job.

• THINGS may mean physical objects, instruments, tools, machinery, equipment, vehicles, materials, and desk-top items such as pencils, paper clips, telephones, stamps, etc.

14 Skills With People,
primarily, though they
also involve information
and things

/\

[14. Working With Animals]
13. Training
12. Counseling (holistic)
11. Advising, Consulting
10. Treating
9. Founding, Leading
8. Negotiating, Deciding
7. Managing, Supervising
6. Performing, Amusing
5. Persuading
4. Communicating
3. Sensing, Feeling
2. Serving
1. Taking Instructions

11 Skills With Things,
primarily, though they may
also involve information

/\

40. Repairing
39. Setting Up
38. Precision Working
37. Operating (vehicles)
36. Operating (equipment)
35. Using (tools)
34. Minding
33. Feeding, Emptying
32. Working With The Earth
   Or Nature
31. Being Athletic
30. Handling (objects)

15 Skills With
Information or Data,
primarily, though they
also involve things

/\

29. Achieving
28. Expediting
27. Planning, Developing
26. Designing
25. Creating, Synthesizing
24. Improving, Adapting
23. Visualizing
22. Evaluating
21. Organizing
20. Analyzing
19. Researching
18. Computing
17. Copying, Storing
   & Retrieving
16. Comparing
15. Observing

● Using the first story we asked you to write, above, you now need to run that story down the list of *possible* skills with PEOPLE, INFORMATION, and then THINGS. Since your possible skills are in all three categories, the Road in this Map now divides into three—

at least temporarily:

YOUR PEOPLE SKILLS
YOUR SKILLS WITH INFORMATION
YOUR SKILLS WITH THINGS

WHAT

• first, the road through skills with PEOPLE, and then
• the road through skills with INFORMATION/DATA, and then
• the road through skills with THINGS.

YOUR FUNCTIONAL/TRANSFERABLE SKILLS INVENTORY

I N S T R U C T I O N S

1.   Get story. Take the story you have just written. It should be on a separate sheet of paper. Give the story some brief title.

2.   Get list. Turn to the next page in this Map. You will see that the road flows by (on the left-hand side) a list of Skills you may have with People.

3.   Read the list, one by one. Put your story's title at the bottom of the page where it says "#1." Then, read over the first People Skill, its definition, and all the skill verbs immediately under it.

4.   Color in. If you feel that in the story in question you used that skill, or any of its variations, *color in* with pen or pencil the appropriate rectangle/square in column #1. For example:

/1 /2 /3 /

---

1. TAKING INSTRUCTIONS
Giving attention to instructions, and then carrying out the prescribed action.
Representing; following through; executing; enforcing regulations; rendering support services.

---

5.   Copy words that apply. *If* you colored in this rectangle/square, it means you feel *some* skill verbs there, apply to you in this story. Choose the ones most meaningful to you, and copy them into the box with the heading, "I am skilled at . . ." Leave plenty of room in that box, as during the succeeding six stories that you will be analyzing eventually, you may want to copy other words for those six.

6.   Adapt the words so they are yours. There is nothing sacred about the skill words on the left-hand side of the page. If you can think of a better way to say what your skill is, *do not hesitate* to put the skill into your own words. Use the *Bank* of Additional Skill-Verbs (to the right of the page) for helpful suggestions.

7.   Work your way on down the page. As you read each skill in turn, do not ask yourself "Do I have this skill?" That is not the issue. The issue is: "Did I use this skill, or any of its variations, in *this* story?" If you can hardly bear to pass by a box, because you *know* you have that skill—even though it was not used in *this* story—think hard of some achievement of yours from the past, where you *did* use that skill. Jot down a reminder to yourself, to use that as your next story. You will be writing seven such stories eventually, remember. Now you know what one to write next. And maybe, before you're through going down this entire list with your first story, you'll get some terrific ideas for the other six.

8.   Turn to page 24. That has to do with Skills you may have with information. Follow the same procedure.

9.   Turn to page 30. That has to do with Skills you may have with Things. Follow the same procedure.

10. You are done with your first story. You have matched it against the 40 major skills that exist in the world of work, and plucked out those that describe you *in that story.* You have also probably gotten an idea of an even better story you could have chosen. Never mind. Just make that one your next story.

11. Write your second story, now. Don't write it *until* now. You see why. As a result of running your first story all the way through this Skills List, you doubtless got a better idea of *what to write, and how* to write it. Take your second story through the same process as the first, now, beginning with writing its title down at the bottom where it says #2, on all three pages.

12. Etc. When you are done analyzing the second story, then write your third. Run it through the same process. Then your fourth. Etc. Etc. Etc. until you are done with all seven.

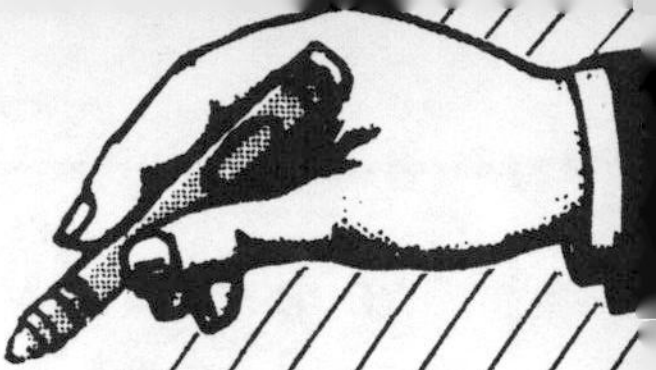

Skills you may have with **People**

Basically thirteen skills, with one additional one that deals with animals

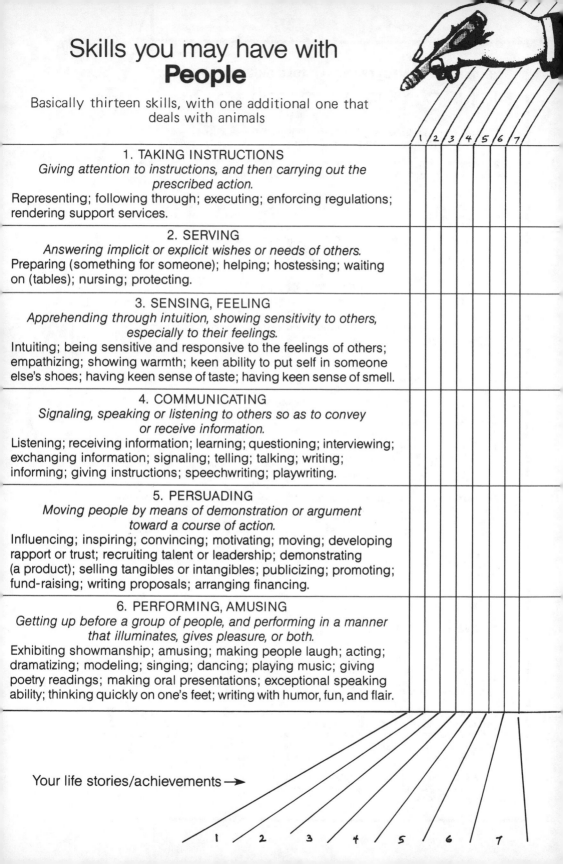

1 2 3 4 5 6 7

1. TAKING INSTRUCTIONS

Giving attention to instructions, and then carrying out the prescribed action.

Representing; following through; executing; enforcing regulations; rendering support services.

2. SERVING

Answering implicit or explicit wishes or needs of others.

Preparing (something for someone); helping; hostessing; waiting on (tables); nursing; protecting.

3. SENSING, FEELING

Apprehending through intuition, showing sensitivity to others, especially to their feelings.

Intuiting; being sensitive and responsive to the feelings of others; empathizing; showing warmth; keen ability to put self in someone else's shoes; having keen sense of taste; having keen sense of smell.

4. COMMUNICATING

Signaling, speaking or listening to others so as to convey or receive information.

Listening; receiving information; learning; questioning; interviewing; exchanging information; signaling; telling; talking; writing; informing; giving instructions; speechwriting; playwriting.

5. PERSUADING

Moving people by means of demonstration or argument toward a course of action.

Influencing; inspiring; convincing; motivating; moving; developing rapport or trust; recruiting talent or leadership; demonstrating (a product); selling tangibles or intangibles; publicizing; promoting; fund-raising; writing proposals; arranging financing.

6. PERFORMING, AMUSING

Getting up before a group of people, and performing in a manner that illuminates, gives pleasure, or both.

Exhibiting showmanship; amusing; making people laugh; acting; dramatizing; modeling; singing; dancing; playing music; giving poetry readings; making oral presentations; exceptional speaking ability; thinking quickly on one's feet; writing with humor, fun, and flair.

Your life stories/achievements →

1 2 3 4 5 6 7

I am skilled at

	Additional Skill-Verbs Bank: Expert at getting things done; ability to follow detailed instructions; ability to implement decisions; unusual ability to represent others.
	Additional Skill-Verbs Bank: Attending to; rendering services to; ministering to; caring for the handicapped; skilled at public relations; dealing patiently with difficult people.
	Additional Skill-Verbs Bank: Developing warmth over the telephone; creating an atmosphere of acceptance; ability to shape atmosphere of a place so that it is warm, pleasant and comfortable; refusing to put people into slots or categories; treating others as equals, without regard to education, authority or position.
	Additional Skill-Verbs Bank: Skilled at striking up conversations with strangers; talks easily with all kinds of people; adept at gathering information from people by talking to them; listening intently and accurately; ability to hear and answer questions perceptively; adept at two-way dialogue; expressing with clarity; verbalizing cogently; responding.
	Additional Skill-Verbs Bank: Expert in reasoning persuasively; influencing the ideas and attitudes of others; making distinctive visual presentations; selling a program or course of action to decision-makers; obtaining agreement after the fact; building customer loyalty; promotional writing; creating imaginative advertising and publicity programs.
	Additional Skill-Verbs Bank: Having strong theatrical sense; understudying; addressing large or small groups confidently; very responsive to audiences' moods or ideas; distracting; diverting; provoking laughter; relating seemingly disparate ideas by means of words or actions; employing humor in describing one's experiences; exceptionally good at facial expressions or body language to express thoughts or feelings eloquently; using voice tone and rhythm as unusually effective tool of communication; giving radio or TV presentations.

Possible skills with People *(CONTINUED)*

	1	2	3	4	5	6	7
7. MANAGING, SUPERVISING *Monitoring individual behavior and coordinating with others',* *for the systematic achieving of some organizational objective.* Determining goals; interpreting goals; promoting harmonious relations & efficiency; encouraging people; coordinating; managing; overseeing; heading; administering; directing public affairs; directing (production of); controlling (a project).							
8. NEGOTIATING, DECIDING *Arriving at an individual or jointly agreed-upon decision,* *usually through discussion and compromise.* Exchanging information; discussing; conferring; working well in a hostile environment; treating people fairly; mediating; arbitrating; bargaining; umpiring; adjudicating; renegotiating; compromising; reconciling; resolving; charting mergers; making policy.							
9. FOUNDING, LEADING *Enlisting and synergizing others toward a corporate objective.* Initiating; originating; founding; instituting; establishing; charting; financing; determining goals, objectives and procedures; recognizing and utilizing the skills of others; enlisting; displaying charisma; inspiring trust; evoking loyalty; organizing diverse people into a group; unifying; synergizing; team-building; sharing responsibility; delegating authority; contracting; taking manageable risks; conducting (music).							
10. TREATING *Acting to improve a physical, mental, emotional or spiritual problem* *of others, by using a specified technique or substance.* Caring for; improving; altering; rehabilitating; having true therapeutic abilities; prescribing; counseling; praying over; curing.							
11. ADVISING, CONSULTING *Giving expert advice or recommendations,* *based on an area of expertise one possesses.* Reading avidly; continually gathering information with respect to a particular problem or area of expertise; offering services; giving expert advice; consulting; trouble-shooting; recommending; referring.							
12. (HOLISTIC) COUNSELING *Dealing with a person's problems in the context of their total self,* *to identify and resolve them through self-directed action.* Advising; counseling; mentoring; facilitating personal growth and development of others; helping people identify their problems, needs, and solutions; interpreting dreams; solving problems; raising people's self-esteem.							

1 2 3 4 5 6 7

I am skilled at	
	Additional Skill-Verbs Bank: Devising systematic approach to goal setting; monitoring behavior through watching, critical evaluation, and feedback; adept at planning and staging ceremonies; planning, organizing and staging of theatrical productions; conducting (music).
	Additional Skill-Verbs Bank: Collaborating with colleagues skillfully; handling prima donnas tactfully and well; handling super-difficult people in situations, without stress; getting diverse groups to work together; expert at liaison roles; adept at conflict management; accepting of differing opinions; arriving at jointly agreed-upon decision or policy or program or solution; promoting and bringing about major policy changes.
	Additional Skill-Verbs Bank: Unusual ability to work self-directedly, without supervision; perceptive in identifying and assessing the potential of others; attracting skilled, competent, and creative people; willing to experiment with new approaches; instinctively understands political realities; recognizing when more information is needed before a decision can be reached; skilled at chairing meetings; deft at directing creative talent; adept at calling in other experts or helpers as needed.
	Additional Skill-Verbs Bank: Making and using contacts effectively; finding and getting things not easy to find; acting as resource broker; giving professional advice; giving insight concerning—
	Additional Skill-Verbs Bank: Helping people make their own discoveries; clarifying values and goals of others; putting things in perspective; adept at confronting others with touchy or difficult personal matters.

Possible skills with People *(CONCLUDED)*

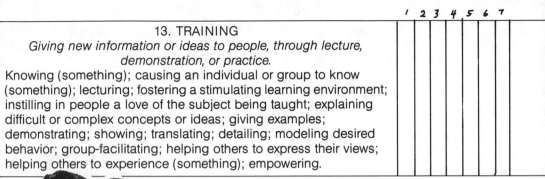

	1	2	3	4	5	6	7

13. TRAINING
Giving new information or ideas to people, through lecture, demonstration, or practice.
Knowing (something); causing an individual or group to know (something); lecturing; fostering a stimulating learning environment; instilling in people a love of the subject being taught; explaining difficult or complex concepts or ideas; giving examples; demonstrating; showing; translating; detailing; modeling desired behavior; group-facilitating; helping others to express their views; helping others to experience (something); empowering.

[14. WORKING WITH ANIMALS]
In general this involves using, with special refinement, the same skills as in the preceding thirteen categories; specifically:
Serving; sensing; communicating; persuading; performing; managing; negotiating; leading; treating; training.

	1	2	3	4	5	6	7

I am skilled at	
	Additional Skill-Verbs Bank: Designing educational events; organizing and administering in-house training events; showing others how to take advantage of a resource; explaining; instructing; enlightening; patient teaching; guiding; tutoring; coaching; using visual communications as teaching aids; interpreting; inventing down-to-earth illustrations for abstract principles or ideas; translating jargon into relevant and meaningful terms, to diverse audiences; speaking a foreign language fluently; teaching a foreign language; skilled at planning and carrying out well-run seminars, workshops or meetings; directing the production of (as, a play).
	Additional Skill-Verbs Bank: Ranching; farming; animal training.

Skills you may have with
Information
Basically fifteen skills

	1	2	3	4	5	6	7

15. OBSERVING
Studying the behavior of people, animals or things,
or the details of a particular phenomenon or place.
Paying careful attention to; being very observant; studying;
concentrating; keeping track of details; focusing on minutiae.

16. COMPARING
Examining two or more people or things,
to discover similarities and dissimilarities.
Comparing; checking; making comparisons; proofreading;
discovering similarities or dissimilarities; perceiving identities
or divergences; developing a standard or model.

17. COPYING, STORING, AND RETRIEVING
Making an imitation in the mind or on various materials.
Entering (data); keeping records; addressing; posting; copying;
transcribing; recording; memorizing; classifying expertly; protecting;
keeping confidential; filing in a way to facilitate retrieval;
remembering; retrieving; extracting; reproducing; imitating;
reviewing; restoring; giving out information patiently and accurately.

18. COMPUTING
Dealing with numbers, performing simple or complex arithmetic.
Counting; taking inventory; calculating; solving statistical problems;
auditing; keeping accurate financial records; reporting; maintaining
fiscal controls; budgeting; projecting; purchasing; operating a
computer competently with spreadsheets and statistics (and, by
extension, with all computer applications: word processing, data-
bases, graphics, and telecommunications).

19. RESEARCHING
Finding and reporting on, things not easy to find.
Investigating; detecting; surveying; inventorying; interviewing;
identifying; finding; gathering; collecting; assembling; compiling;
composing; collating; tabulating; classifying; ascertaining;
determining; proving; disproving; reporting.

20. ANALYZING
Breaking a principle or thing into its constituent parts,
or basic elements.
Examining; visualizing; reasoning; finding the basic units;
dissecting; extracting; selecting; testing; evaluating; perceiving
and defining cause-and-effect relations; proving; interpreting.

Your life stories/achievements ➔

1	2	3	4	5	6	7

I am skilled at	
	Additional Skill-Verbs Bank: Being keenly aware of surroundings; being highly observant of people or data or things; studies other people's behavior perceptively.
	Additional Skill-Verbs Bank: Keeping superior minutes of meetings; having a keen and accurate memory for detail; recalling people and their preferences accurately; retentive memory for rules and procedures; expert at remembering numbers and statistics accurately, and for a long period; having exceedingly accurate melody recognition; exhibiting keen tonal memory; accurately reproducing sounds or tones (e.g., a foreign language, spoken without accent); keeping confidences; keeping secrets; encrypting.
	Additional Skill-Verbs Bank: Performing rapid and accurate manipulation of numbers, in one's head or on paper; preparing financial reports; estimating; ordering; acquiring.
	Additional Skill-Verbs Bank: Relentlessly curious; reading ceaselessly; adept at finding information by interviewing people; discovering; getting; obtaining; reporting accurately; briefing; acting as a resource broker.
	Additional Skill-Verbs Bank: Debating; figuring out; critiquing.

Possible skills with Information *(CONTINUED)*

	1	*2*	*3*	*4*	*5*	*6*	*7*
21. ORGANIZING *Giving a definite structure and working order to things.* Forming into a whole with connected and interdependent parts; collating; formulating; defining; classifying materials; arranging according to a prescribed plan or evolving schema; expertly systematizing.							
22. EVALUATING *Making judgments about people, information, or things.* Diagnosing; inspecting; checking; testing; perceiving common denominators; weighing; appraising; assessing; deciding; judging; screening out people; discriminating what is important from what is unimportant; discarding the unimportant; editing; simplifying; summarizing; consolidating.							
23. VISUALIZING *Able to conceive shapes or sounds, perceiving their patterns and structures, and to enable others to see them too.* Having form perception; imagining; able to visualize shapes; perceiving patterns and structures; skilled at symbol formation; creating poetic images; visualizing concepts; possessing accurate spatial memory; easily remembering faces; having an uncommonly fine sense of rhythm; estimating (e.g., speed); illustrating; photographing; sketching; drawing; coloring; painting; designing; drafting; mapping.							
24. IMPROVING, ADAPTING *Taking what others have developed, and applying it to new situations, often in a new form.* Adjusting; improvising; expanding; improving; arranging (as, music); redesigning; updating; applying.							
25. CREATING, SYNTHESIZING *Transforming apparently unrelated things or ideas, by forming them into a new cohesive whole.* Relating; combining; integrating; unifying; producing a clear, coherent unity; intuiting; inventing; innovating; conceptualizing; hypothesizing; discovering; conceiving new interpretations, concepts and approaches; formulating; programming; projecting; forecasting.							
26. DESIGNING *Fashioning or shaping things.* Creating (things); designing in wood or other media; experimenting; fashioning; shaping; making models; making handicrafts; sculpting; creating symbols.							
	1	*2*	*3*	*4*	*5*	*6*	*7*

I am skilled at	
	Additional Skill-Verbs Bank: Bringing order out of chaos, with masses of physical things; putting into working order.
	Additional Skill-Verbs Bank: Problem-solving; making decisions; eliminating; screening applicants; reducing the size of the database; separating the wheat from the chaff; reviewing large amounts of material and extracting its essence; writing a precis; making fiscal reductions; conserving; upgrading.
	Additional Skill-Verbs Bank: Having a photographic memory; having a memory for design; ability to visualize in three dimensions; conceiving symbolic and metaphoric pictures of reality; possessing color discrimination of a very high order; possessing instinctively excellent taste in design, arrangement and color; skilled at mechanical drawing; able to read blueprints; graphing and reading graphs.
	Additional Skill-Verbs Bank: Making practical applications of theoretical ideas; deriving applications from other people's ideas; able to see the commercial possibilities in a concept, idea or product.
	Additional Skill-Verbs Bank: Having conceptual ability of a high order; being an idea man or woman; having 'ideaphoria'; demonstrating originality; continually conceiving, generating and developing innovative and creative ideas; excellent at problem-solving; creative imagining; possessed of great imagination; improvising on the spur of the moment; developing; estimating; predicting; cooking new creative recipes; composing (music).
	Additional Skill-Verbs Bank: Devising; developing; generating; skilled at symbol formation.

Possible skills with Information *(CONCLUDED)*

27. PLANNING, DEVELOPING
Determining the sequence of tasks, after reviewing pertinent data or requirements, and often overseeing the carrying out of the plan.
Reviewing pertinent data requirements; determining the need for revisions of goals, policies and procedures; planning on the basis of lessons from the past; determining the sequence of operations; making arrangements for the functioning of a system; overseeing; establishing; executing decisions reached; developing, building markets for ideas or products; traveling.

28. EXPEDITING
Speeding up the accomplishment of a task or series of tasks, so as to reach an organizational objective on or ahead of time.
Dispatching; adept at finding ways to speed up a job; establishing effective priorities among competing requirements; skilled at allocating scarce financial resources; setting up and maintaining on-time work schedules; coordinating operations and details; quickly sizing up situations; anticipating people's needs; acting on new information immediately; seeks and seizes opportunities; deals well with the unexpected or critical event; able to make hard decisions; bringing projects in on time and within budget.

29. ACHIEVING
Systematically accomplishing tasks in a manner that causes objectives to be attained or surpassed.
Completing; attaining objectives; winning; meeting goals; producing results; delivering as promised; improving performance; making good use of feedback; increasing productivity.

1 2 3 4 5 6 7

I am skilled at

m. f ley.	Face of Pulley.	Diam. of Flange.	Length of Shaft.	Diam. of Shaft.	Size of Hole in Saw.	Price of each. c'mp'e ft.
in.	3½ in.	2½ in.	16 in.	1 1/16 in.	1 in.	$ 5.50
in.	4½ in.	3 in.	19 in.	1 3/16 in.	1⅛ in.	6.40
in.	4½ in.	3½ in.	20 in.	1 5/16 in.	1¼ in.	6.80
in.	5 in.	4 in.	24 in.	1 7/16 in.	1 5/16 in.	7.80
in.	5¼ in.	4½ in.	26 in.	1 7/16 in.	1⅝ in.	8.80
in.		in.	28 in.	1 7/8 in.	1¾ in.	10.00
				1 7/16 in.	1⅜ in.	11.00
						12.40
						17.20
						20.60

8978 Single throat. 2 ft.
8979 Single throat. 2½ ft.
48980 Single throat. 3 ft.
48981 Single throat. 4½ ft.

Additional Skill-Verbs Bank: Organizes one's time expertly; able to handle a variety of tasks and responsibilities simultaneously and efficiently; continually searches for more responsibility; forecasting; instinctively gathering resources even before the need for them becomes clear; recognizing obsolescence of ideas or procedures before compelling data is yet at hand; anticipating problems or needs before they become problems; decisive in emergencies.

Skills you may have with
Things

Basically eleven skills

	1	2	3	4	5	6	7

30. HANDLING (OBJECTS)
Using one's hands or body to identify or move an object.
Feeling; fingering; washing; raising; lifting; carrying; balancing; pushing; pulling; moving; taking; gathering; receiving; setting (down); shipping; unloading; separating; sorting; distributing; delivering; supplying.

31. BEING ATHLETIC
Using one's body as an instrument of accomplishment.
Displaying great physical agility; possessing great strength; demonstrating outstanding endurance; maintaining uncommon physical fitness; having excellent eye-hand-foot coordination; possessing fine motor coordination.

32. WORKING WITH THE EARTH AND NATURE
Using earth's body as an instrument of accomplishment, though under the limitations of the special laws that are written into the behavior of the earth and growing things.
Clearing; digging; plowing; tilling; seeding; planting; helping to grow; nurturing; weeding; harvesting.

33. FEEDING, EMPTYING (MACHINES)
Putting materials into or taking them out of machines, often as they are running.
Placing; stacking; loading; feeding; emptying; dumping; removing; disposing of.

34. MINDING (MACHINES)
Monitoring, adjusting, and servicing automatic machines, usually as they are running.
Monitoring machines or valves; watching to make sure nothing is wrong; tending; pushing buttons; starting; flipping switches; adjusting controls; turning knobs; stopping; making adjustments when machine threatens to malfunction, or does.

Your life stories/achievements →

1   2   3   4   5   6   7

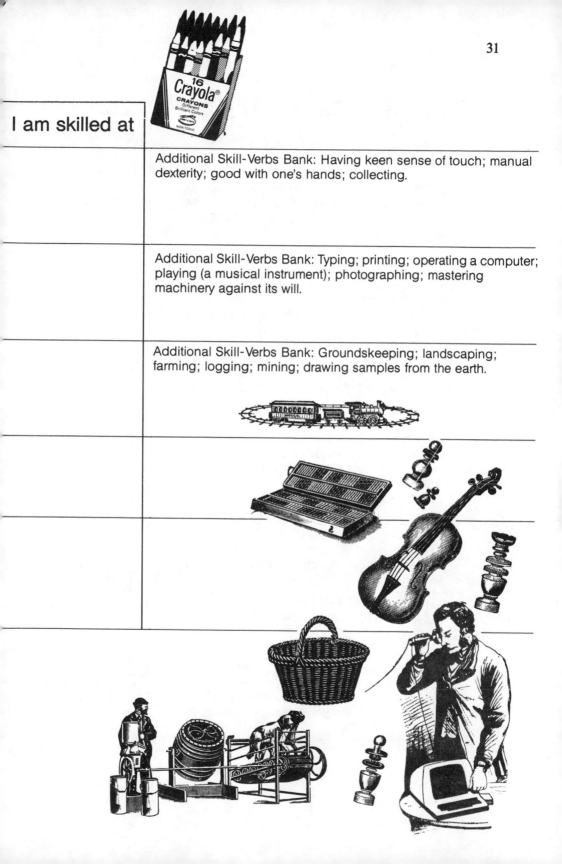

I am skilled at

Additional Skill-Verbs Bank: Having keen sense of touch; manual dexterity; good with one's hands; collecting.

Additional Skill-Verbs Bank: Typing; printing; operating a computer; playing (a musical instrument); photographing; mastering machinery against its will.

Additional Skill-Verbs Bank: Groundskeeping; landscaping; farming; logging; mining; drawing samples from the earth.

Possible skills with Things *(CONCLUDED)*

35. USING (TOOLS) *Manipulating hand tools (electrically-powered or not)* *to accomplish that which the hands by themselves cannot.* The following skills are all accomplished with the aid of kitchen, garden or shop hand tools: using or utilizing (particular tools); manipulating (materials); working; eating; placing; guiding; moving; shaping; molding; filling; cutting; applying; pressing; binding; sewing (by hand); weaving; knitting; painting.							
36. OPERATING (EQUIPMENT OR MACHINES) *Performing some or all of the following operations upon a* *particular kind of (office, shop or other) machine or equipment.* You need to specify which equipment or machines you know how to perform these operations on (e.g., a computer or typewriter); and which operations: starting; operating; inputting; inserting; controlling; maintaining; monitoring; observing; checking; regulating; adjusting; changing; cleaning; refilling; producing (some kind of output, or product).							
37. OPERATING (VEHICLES) *Performing some or all of the following operations* *upon a particular kind of vehicle.* Driving; piloting; navigating; guiding; steering; regulating controls of; switching.							
38. PRECISION WORKING *Precise attainment of set limits, tolerances or standards.* Keypunching; drilling; sandblasting; grinding; forging; fitting; tuning; adjusting; having great finger dexterity; sketching; drawing; painting; sewing minute stitches; making miniatures; skilled at working in the micro-universe.							
39. SETTING UP (DISPLAYS, MACHINERY, EQUIPMENT) Preparing; clearing; laying; constructing; building; assembling; installing; displaying.							
40. REPAIRING *Putting something back into something like its original condition;* *or at least into good operating condition.* You will need to say what it is that you are good at repairing or restoring: fixing; repairing; doing preventative maintenance; trouble-shooting; restoring (as, art).							
	1	2	3	4	5	6	7

I am skilled at

Additional Skill-Verbs Bank: Typing; printing; operating a computer; playing (a musical instrument); mastering machinery against its will.

Additional Skill-Verbs Bank: Giving continuous attention to the vehicle; offering a ready response to any emergency.

Additional Skill-Verbs Bank: Having great dexterity with small instruments (as, tweezers).

Now, You Need Priorities

Well, you did it. Seven stories all done. And analyzed for their skills. You've got a nice list called "I am skilled at..." Good going!

Now what? Well, unfortunately, this new list of your skills *will do you absolutely no good if you do not then go on to say which skill you like best, which next best, etc.*

Why? Because, until you can say *that,* you can't even begin to define "Your Ideal Job or Career." *Almost every* job demands that you have skills with People, Information and Things—in one degree or another. It's that *degree* that determines *which* job or career we're talking about.

To define your next job or career you *must* prioritize your skills. Without this essential step, you will get bogged down for sure.

This prioritizing has two levels to it:

I. What you first need to know about yourself is: "Which kinds of skills do I most enjoy using? Those with People? Or those with Information? Or those with Things? Or, if all three, which is most important to me, which is next most important, and which is least important?" What career or job you choose next, will depend upon this discovery and this decision of yours, more than any other. Don't ever underestimate the importance of the distinction between PEOPLE, INFORMATION, and THINGS. It is the key to everything.

II. Then, within the three broad families of Skills (People, Information and Things), you MUST decide *which* "People Skills," and *which* "Information Skills," and *which* "Things Skills" are most important to you.

How Do You Prioritize? You begin by just trusting your intuition. Look over your colored-in pages: People, Information, and Things. Which skills do you like most to use, of the three? People? Information? or Things? Of the three, which is next? Which is your least favorite?

Next: look at the "People Skills" pages, all by themselves. Look at the skills you wrote down, in the "I am skilled at..." sections. On a separate piece of paper, copy these with your favorite at the top, your least favorite at the bottom. Cross out (or omit) any skills *you have* but don't enjoy using. You are only looking for *enjoy* here.

You may be able to do this prioritizing just by common sense. If not, use the "Prioritizing Grid" that you will find in the next section of this Map—under "Special Knowledges"—to help you.

When you are done with your "People Skills," turn to the "Information Skills" pages, and follow the same procedure. Use a new piece of blank paper. Get all your "Information Skills"—in the "I am skilled at..." sections—written down on this blank paper, in the order of their exact priority for you. Again, omit any skills you don't truly enjoy using.

When you are done with your "Information Skills," turn to the "Things Skills" pages, and again follow the same procedure, using a new piece of blank paper. Get your "Things Skills" too, into exact priority. And, once again, omit any skills you don't truly enjoy using.

NOW you have some truly useful information.

Incidentally, on page 52 you will find a place to *summarize* your findings. There is a picture of a Tree, there. And on the left-hand side of that tree, is a place for you to write your favorite *top three* or four "People Skills," AND your favorite *top three* or four "Information Skills," AND your favorite *top three* or four "Things Skills." Do save the papers, however, on which you have written out *all* your favorite People Skills, etc. For now, the *top three* of each, will do. But later, you may want to go back and look at the rest of the list.

Where

Where You Want to Use Your Skills

14,000,000 Job Markets. Jobhunters begin by thinking there are too few job markets (and therefore, too few jobs) "out there." We argue just the opposite. There are too many. If you try to hit them all (shotgun style) you will only diffuse your energies and your effectiveness.

It is, of course, nice to 'stay loose' and be willing to use your skills any place that there is a vacancy. Unfortunately, experts say that 80% of all the vacancies which occur in this country, above entry level, are never advertised through any of the channels or avenues that job-hunters traditionally turn to.

So, you're going to have to approach any place and every place that looks attractive to you.

Thus, you can't rule out any place that looks interesting to you, because it's just possible they have a vacancy that you don't know about. Or will develop one *while you're there*. Or will decide (since they may be expanding) to create a job just for you.

You can't, of course, go visit EVERY place that looks interesting. Hence, the importance of this part of your homework. You've GOT to "cut the territory down" to some manageable size, by using:

Some Principles of Exclusion For Narrowing Down The Area You Need To Focus On

YOU START WITH
THE WHOLE JOB-MARKET IN THIS COUNTRY—

1 You narrow this down by deciding just what area, city or county you want to work in. This leaves you with however many thousands of job markets there are in that area or city. **2** You narrow this down by identifying your Strongest Skills, on their highest level that you can legitimately claim, and then thru research deciding what field you *want* to work in, above all. This leaves you with all the hundreds of businesses/community organizations/ agencies/schools/hospitals/projects/associations/ foundations/institutions/firms or government agen- cies there are in that area and in the field you have chosen. **3** You narrow this down by get- ting acquainted with the economy in the area thru personal interviews with various contacts; and supplementing this with study of journals in your field, in order that you can pinpoint the places that interest you the most. This leaves a manageable num- ber of markets for you to do some study on. **4** You now narrow this down by asking yourself: *Can I be happy in this place, and do they have the kind of problems which my strongest skills can help solve for them?* **5** This leaves you with the companies or or- ganizations which you will now care- fully plan how to approach for a job, in your case, *the* job.

Some Principles of Exclusion For Narrowing Down The Area You Need To Focus On

1 **Special Knowledges.** The First Principle for Narrowing Down the Organizations You Will Need to Take A Look At: WHAT SPECIAL KNOWLEDGES DO YOU WANT TO BE ABLE TO USE ON THE JOB?

Set Up A Form. Here you will need another blank sheet of paper. Divide it into four columns, and put the following headings on those columns:
1. Special Knowledges I Picked Up In School or College.
2. Special Knowledges I Picked Up On The Job, Or Just By Doing (At Home or Work).
3. Special Knowledges I Picked Up From Seminars or Workshops, Etc.
4. Special Knowledges I Picked Up Just By Reading Avidly Or Talking With People.

Down the left-hand side, you can put the Years, working back from the present, in five-year increments: e.g., 1985-1981, 1980-1976, 1975-1971, etc.

List the Knowledges You Have. Now you are ready to start filling it in. Using your memory, or borrowing that of a longstanding friend, list EVERY knowledge you have ever picked up anywhere. Examples would be as follows:

Circle the Ones You Love. When you are all done with *your* list (not mine), go back and *circle* all the knowledges you would *love* to be able to use in your next job or career.

Put Them in Priority. Then, choose your top ten, and get them into *exact order*—from most favorite, to least favorite. Use the "Prioritizing Grid" on the next page, in order to help you do this.

(You will, incidentally, need to go to a copying machine first and make several copies of this Prioritizing Grid, inasmuch as you will be using it in each of these "Where" exercises.)

Special Knowledges I Picked Up In School or College	Special Knowledges I Picked Up On The Job, Or Just By Doing (At Home or Work)	Special Knowledges I Picked Up From Seminars, or Workshops, Etc.	Special Knowledges I Picked Up Just By Reading Avidly Or Talking With People
Spanish; Psychology; Biology; Geometry; Accounting; Music appreciation; Sociology.	How to Operate a computer; How a volunteer organization works; Principles of financial planning and management.	The way the brain works; Principles of art; Speed reading; Drawing on the right side of the brain.	How computers work; Principles of comparison shopping; Principles of outdoor survival; Knowledge of antiques.

Prioritizing Grid

For Ten Items. Here is a method for taking (say) 10 items, and figuring out which one is most important to you, which is next most important, etc.:

List, Compare. Make a list of the items and number them. *In the case of Specific Knowledges, make a list of the ten subjects you know the most about, then number them 1 thru 10.* Now, look at the top line of this grid. You see a 1 and 2 there. So, compare items one and two on your list. Which one is more important to you? *State the question any way you want to: in the case of Specific Knowledges, you might ask yourself: if I was being offered two jobs, one which used knowledge #1, and one which used #2, other things being equal, which would I prefer?* Circle it. Then go on to the next pair, etc.

1 2								
1 3	2 3							
1 4	2 4	3 4						
1 5	2 5	3 5	4 5					
1 6	2 6	3 6	4 6	5 6				
1 7	2 7	3 7	4 7	5 7	6 7			
1 8	2 8	3 8	4 8	5 8	6 8	7 8		
1 9	2 9	3 9	4 9	5 9	6 9	7 9	8 9	
1 10	2 10	3 10	4 10	5 10	6 10	7 10	8 10	9 10

Circle, Count. Total Times Each Number Got Circled:

1 ___ 2 ___ 3 ___ 4 ___ 5 ___ 6 ___ 7 ___ 8 ___ 9 ___ 10 ___

When you are all done, count up the number of times each number got circled, all told. Enter these totals in the spaces just above.

Recopy. Finally, recopy your list, beginning with the item that got the most circles. This is your *new #1.* Then the item that got the next most circles. This is your *new #2.*

In case of a tie (two numbers got the same number of circles), look back on the grid to see when you were comparing those two numbers there, which one got circled. That means you prefer That One over the other; thus you break the tie.

P.S. If you need to compare any list that has more than 10 items to it, just keep adding new rows to the bottom of the grid. Thus: 1 *11* 2 *11,* etc. Until you have all the numbers compared.

Copy this Prioritized List. When you are done, copy the 10 in their exact order of priority now on that (formerly) blank sheet of paper—one side or the other—that you have been working on.

Summarize It On The Tree Diagram. Turn to page 52 once again, if you will, and in the place provided there on the left-hand side of the Tree, put your top four or five Special Knowledges.

If You Want To Do Several Different Part-Time Jobs. If you want to have a Composite Career—combining two or three different jobs into one Career—copy the picture of the Tree onto more than one larger pieces of paper. Have a separate Tree for each separate career or job, and put different skills and different Special Knowledges (from your prioritized list) on separate Tree diagrams. Do remember, however, to save the paper that you have been copying from. It may be you will want to consult it later, to see where you might use the rest of your favorite special knowledges—in your leisure, for example.

The Second Principle For Narrowing Down The Organizations You Will Want To Take A Look At:

2 **WHAT DO YOU WANT THE GOALS OF THE ORGANIZATION TO BE, WHERE YOU WILL BE WORKING?**

A Product, A Service, or Information? That's the first question. Do you dodge this question by saying simply, "I want to work for a place that makes money." The response is: "Makes money doing WHAT?" We are back to the question above: Do you want to work in a place (of your own choosing or your own devising) whose goal is to produce a product? Or, would you prefer to work in a place whose goal is to render some kind of service to people? Or, would you prefer to work in a place whose business it is to get information out to people?

You have to make a decision about the goals of the organization NOW or later. You can postpone it. But you cannot evade it.

If You Choose a Product, What *Kind* of Product? What kind of product do you want the place to be *producing,* OR what kind of product do you want to be able to *work with, or use,* at this place? Either answer will help you narrow down the kinds of places. If, for example, you say, "I want to work at a place where I could use a drill press," that will help narrow down the places you need to take a look at, in your given city or area.

So, read over this list, and circle any products/things/whatever that interest you and that you would like to work with, *or* help produce. (Do say which, please.)

Machines
Tools
Toys
Equipment
Products
Desk-top
 supplies
Crops, plants,
 trees
Dollies,
 handtrucks
Boxes
Automatic
 machines
Paper
Laundry
Dishes, pots
 and pans
Controls,
 gauges
Copying
 machines
PBX switch-
 boards
Valves, switches,
 buttons
Computer
Tables
Portable power
 tools
Kitchen and
 garden tools
Meats
Typewriters
Mimeograph
 machines
TV camera
Vehicles
Transparencies
Therapy center
Cranks, wheels,
 gears, levers
Hoists, cranes
Matches
Candles
Lanterns,
 oil lamps
Light bulbs
Fluorescent
 lights
Laser beams
Windmills
Waterwheels
Water turbines

Gas turbines
Steam turbines
Steam engines
Fuel cells
Batteries
Transformers,
 electric motors,
 dynamos
Engines, gas,
 diesel
Dynamite
Nuclear reactors
Other things
 belonging to
 the field of
 Energy:
Electronic
 devices
Electronic
 games
Calculators
Lie detectors
Radar
 equipment
Clocks
Telescopes
Microscopes
X-ray machines
Pens, ink, felt-tip,
 ballpoint
Pencils, black,
 red or other
Printing presses,
 type, ink
Woodcuts,
 engravings,
 lithographs
Paintings,
 drawings,
 silk-screens
Books
Braille
Newspapers
Magazines
Teleprinters
Telephones
Telegraphs
Radios
Records
Phonographs
Stereos
Tape recorders
Cameras
Movies

Television sets
Video recorders
Games
Amusements
Cards
Board games,
 checkers,
 chess, etc.
Kites
Gambling
 devices or
 machines
Musical
 instruments
Money
Cash registers
Financial
 records
Roads
Bicycles
Motorcycles
Mopeds
Cars
Parking meters
Traffic lights
Railways
Subways
Canals
Boats
Steamships
Gliders
Airplanes
Parachutes
Balloons
Foods
Food
 preservatives
Artificial foods
Health foods
Vitamins
Can openers
Refrigerators
Microwave ovens
Wells
Cisterns
Bathtubs
Soaps
Umbrellas
Clothing
Spinning wheels,
 looms

Patterns, safety
 pins, buttons,
 zippers
Dyes
Cloths
Sewing
 machines
Shoes
Beds
Furniture
Sheets, blankets,
 electric blankets
Towels
Washing
 machines,
 dryers
Wash-day
 products,
 bleach
Cosmetics
Toiletries
Drugs
Cigarettes
Tents
Plywood
Bricks
Cement
Concrete
Cinder-block
Carpenters' tools
Chimneys
Columns
Domes
Paint
Wallpaper
Heating
 elements,
 furnaces
Carpeting
Fire
 extinguishers
Fire alarms
Burglar alarms
Crafts-materials
Paper-mache
Hides
Pottery
Pewter
Paraffin, pitch
Bronze, brass
Cast iron,
 ironworks

Steel, aluminum
Rubber
Plastics
Textiles
Felt
Synthetics
Elastic
Gym equipment
Medicines
Vaccines
Anesthetics
Thermometers
Hearing aids
Dental drills
False parts
 of human body
Spectacles,
 glasses,
 contacts
Fishing rods,
 fishhooks, bait
Traps, guns
Beehives
Ploughs
Fertilizers
Pesticides
Weed killers
Threshing
 machines,
 reapers,
 harvesters
Shovels
Picks
Lawnmowers
Dairy equipment
Wine-making
 equipment
Bottles
Cans

When you're done with the list, PLEASE prioritize it. Put the products in order, from your most favorite to your least favorite. Use the "Prioritizing Grid."

If You Choose A Service, What *Kind* of Service? Do you want to service or repair some kind of product? If so, review the list above, please—with that in mind. Copy down what sort of product you would like to service.

Is the kind of service you want to offer related to helping people with some kind of personal problem? If so, what kind of people, and what kind of problem? Here is a list, to get your imagination going. Circle any that enchant you.

People needing help with the following special problems:
- Life adjustment or life/work planning
- Unemployment or job-hunting
- Being fired or laid-off
- Stress
- Relationships
  - Shyness
  - Meeting people, starting friendships
  - Complaints, grievances
  - Anger   Rape
  - Love   Abuse
  - Marriage   Parenting
  - Sex   Divorce
- Possessions
  - Personal economics
  - Budgeting
  - Debt, bankruptcy
  - Financial planning
- Problems Generally Regarded As Related Primarily to the Mind
  - Mental retardation
  - Personal insight, therapy
  - Communications, thoughts-feelings
  - Illiteracy, educational needs
  - Industry's in-house training
- Problems Generally Regarded As Related Primarily to the 'Heart' (Beauty, Feelings, etc.)
  - Expressed feelings
  - Learning how to love
  - Self-acceptance and acceptance of others
  - Boredom
  - Loneliness
  - Anxiety
  - Fear
  - Anger
  - Depression
  - Mental illness
  - Psychiatric hospitalization
  - Death and grief

- Problems Generally Regarded As Related Primarily to the 'Will' (Perfection, Ethics, Actions, Doing)
  - Prescribed actions
  - Competing needs
  - Performance problems, appraisal
  - Discipline problems, self-discipline
  - Personal powerlessness
  - Work satisfaction
  - Values
  - Ethics
  - Philosophy or religion
- Problems Generally Regarded As Related Primarily to the Body
  - Physical handicaps
  - Physical fitness
  - Sexual dysfunction
  - Pregnancy and childbirth
  - Overweight
  - Nutritional problems
  - Low energy
  - Allergies
  - Sleep disorders
  - Hypertension
  - Pain
  - Disease in general
  - Terminal illness
  - Self-healing, psychic healing
  - Treatment or drug addiction
  - Alcoholism
  - Smoking

[*As the line between psyche and soma is very thin, many will prefer all or some of the listings immediately above to be listed under "the mind," rather than under "the body."*]

- Problems Generally Regarded As Related Primarily to the 'Spirit'
  - Religion
  - Stewardship
  - Worship
  - Psychic phenomena
  - Life after death
- Problems Regarded by Some as Holistic— Embracing Body, Spirit, Mind, Heart and Will
  - Any of the above may be so-regarded
  - Holistic health
  - Holistic medicine or healing

What Kinds of People Would You Most Like to Work With? Underline or circle any descriptions below that are a part of your answer to this question.

Individuals	People in their thirties
Groups of eight or less	The middle-aged
Groups larger than eight	The elderly
Babies	All people of all ages
School-age children	Men
Adolescents or	Women
young people	Heterosexuals
College students	Homosexuals
Young adults	All people regardless
	of sex

People of a particular cultural background

(Namely, ———————————————)

People of a particular economic background

(Namely, ———————————————)

People of a particular social background

(Namely, ———————————————)

People of a particular educational background

(Namely, ———————————————)

People of a particular philosophy or religious belief

(Namely, ———————————————)

Certain kinds of workers (blue-collar, white-collar, executives, or whatever)

(Namely, ———————————————)

People who are powerless

(Namely, ———————————————)

People who wield power (e.g., opinion-makers, etc.)

(Namely, ———————————————)

People who are easy to work with
People who are difficult to work with
  ("a challenge," as we say: i.e., prima donnas)
People in a particular place (the Armed
  Services, prison, etc.)

(Namely, ———————————————).

When you're done with the list, PLEASE prioritize it. Put the services in order, from your most favorite to your least favorite. Also, the kind of people you would like to serve. Again, don't hesitate to copy and use the "Prioritizing Grid."

If You Choose To Work For An Organization That Collects or Dispenses Information, What *Kind* of Information or Data? You may already know. Instantly. No need to work through the list below at all. On the other hand, maybe you know that you like to work with information—but you're not clear about what kind of information. If so, go over the list below, and circle the sorts of things you *love* to work with—or *would* love to work with:

Data in General

Knowledge	Words
Conceptions or	Symbols
ideas or theories	Facts
Numbers or	Information
statistics	History

Data Primarily Dealing With Things

Parameters	Designs
Boundary conditions	Blueprints
Frameworks	Wall-charts
Specifications	Time-charts
Precision requirements	Schema
Principles	Schematic analyses
Principles' applications	Techniques
Standards	Methods
Repeating requirements	Procedures
Variables	Specialized procedures

Data Primarily Dealing With People

Many of the above may be so-regarded or used. Also:

Intangibles	Objectives
Intuitions	Goals
Sequences	Project goals
Solutions	Tactical needs
New approaches	Needs
Public moods	Organizational contexts
Opinion-collection	Operations
Points of view	Systems
Sources	Work assignments
Programs	Reporting systems
Projects	Controls systems
Surveys	Performance character-
Investigations	istics
Research projects	Proficiencies
Research and develop-	Deficiencies
ment projects	Records management
Inputs	Catalogs
Outputs	Handbooks
Reports	Trade or professional
Conclusions	literature
Findings	Data analysis studies
Recommendations	Statistical analyses
Policy recommendations	Financial needs
Policy formulations	Costs
Plans	Accountings

When you're done with the list, PLEASE prioritize it. Put the types of information in order, from your most favorite to your least favorite. Again, don't hesitate to copy and use the "Prioritizing Grid."

Summarize It All, On Your Tree Diagram. Turn to page 52 once again, if you will, and in the place provided there on the left-hand side of the Tree, put your summary of 'GOALS OF THE ORGANIZATION.' It should state whether Product, Service, Information or any fourth alternative that you made up. And *which* kind, in specifics.

Combine Wherever Possible. It doesn't have to be Product OR Service OR Information. It can be any two of the above. Or any three. For example, you might decide that the kind of Information you would most like to get out to people would be a catalog. Fine, but then if that's the only thing you can say about yourself, you're going to have to cover every place in your entire 'target' geographical area, that produces a catalog of some sort. If however, you discovered that on the Product list, you liked the idea of Gym Equipment, that should be added to "catalog." It now reads "Producing catalogs of gym equipment." *That* narrows down the field in a much more satisfactory manner. You now have a *manageable* number of places to locate, investigate, and visit.

The Third Principle For Narrowing Down The Organizations You Will Want To Take A Look At:

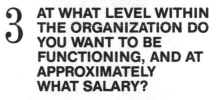

3 AT WHAT LEVEL WITHIN THE ORGANIZATION DO YOU WANT TO BE FUNCTIONING, AND AT APPROXIMATELY WHAT SALARY?

You've GOT to make some decisions about this, at some point. For, your answer to this question will determine at what level you do your investigating, in the "HOW" section of this Map.

Here are some of the possible levels you may choose from: Volunteer • Intern • Entry-level worker • One who supervises others • One who works essentially alone •

One who works with one other, in tandem • One who works as a member of a team • The head of the organization • The founder of the organization.

The salary you desire will also influence the level at which your "HOW" investigation will proceed. See Chapter Seven in *What Color Is Your Parachute?* for guidance in stating your desires about salary.

Summarize It All, On Your Tree Diagram. Turn to page 52 once again, if you will, and in the place provided there on the left-hand side of the Tree, put your summary of "LEVEL AND SALARY DESIRED."

Good.

You now have all the basic raw materials for finding out what your ideal future job might be.

But What About The *Right* Side Of The Tree Diagram? Ah, yes. There *are* three more "principles of exclusion." *However,* these will *probably* only be useful to you *after* you have narrowed your search down to three or four places that truly interest you; and you are then trying to make up your mind between them.

At that point you will need some further principles of exclusion, to narrow down the territory. At that point, "working conditions," and "types of people you will be working with," and "preferred geography factors" will help you decide.

The Fourth Principle For Narrowing Down The Organizations,—Usually *After* You've Taken A Look At Them:

4 WHAT KINDS OF WORKING CONDITIONS DO YOU WANT?

Figure Out What's Important To You. *When* you are looking at, and weighing, two or more organizations, you will be able to give preference to one above the others *if* you know *under what conditions you do your best work.* This can include *anything!* Such as:

- Do you prefer work outdoors, or indoors?
- Do you want to work for an organization with 20 or less employees? 100 or more? 500 or more? 1000 or more?
- Do you want to work in a place where you know everyone, or not?
- Do you want to work in a room with windows, or don't you care?
- Do you want to be working in close physical proximity to others, or not?
- What distasteful working conditions from your past do you want to be SURE not to repeat?
- What kind of dress code, supervision, use of authority, openness to change, do you want to have—in order to do your most effective work?

Write these answers out on a separate piece of blank paper.

Prioritize The List. Then (you know by now): PRIORITIZE the list, using another copy of the "Prioritizing Grid."

Summarize It On The Tree Diagram. Turn to page 53, and enter your top five answers in the appropriate place on the right-hand side of the Tree diagram. As you stare at it, it will *of course* occur to you that *some* of the list here *may be useful to you before* you begin your search. For example, if you decide you want to work for an organization with 20 or less employees, *that* will be an important principle to have in hand *before* you begin your search—as it will determine *which* organizations you focus your attention on.

Generally speaking, however, as we said earlier, these "preferred working conditions" will be more useful to you after you have three or four particular organizations in mind.

The Fifth Principle For Narrowing Down The Organizations,—Usually *After* You've Taken A Look

5 WHAT KINDS OF PEOPLE WOULD YOU LIKE TO BE WORKING WITH?

WHAT "Kinds of People" usually means two things. *What kinds of people do you want to be dealing with as clients, customers, consumers, students, or whatever?* AND: *What kinds of people do you want to have working beside you within your organization? beside you, with you, under you, and over you?*

Who Do You Want To Serve? The answer to the first part lies in the list we saw, back when we were dealing with WHAT KINDS OF SERVICES DO YOU WANT TO OFFER, AND TO WHOM? If you need help here, now, go back and look at that list. It should give you some helpful starts toward this subject.

Who Do You Want Beside You? As for "the kinds of people you would like to have working beside you, within your organization"—all you have to do is take a blank piece of paper and make a list of all the kinds of people you have already worked with (at home or at work), and hope you will never have to work with again.

Negatives Into Positives. Then turn those "negative" factors into "positive factors"—which will often, but not always, be their opposites.

Prioritize the list (of course) and you will have a splendid list of what to look for. When at a later point in your job-hunt you have three or four places under consideration, and they look rather equally attractive to you, *this* list will separate the men from the boys, and the women from the girls. Also the sheep from the goats.

Here Come Your Values. *Most often* you will discover that "Types of People" is utterly dependent upon your "value system." You would call them your "traits." In the jargon of vocational experts, they are called "Self Management Skills." Whatever the language, we are obviously referring to all those traits (or skills) that you were missing seeing in the WHAT part of this Map. Traits/skills such as these:

Some Typical Self-Management Skills/Traits

A
Adept(ness)
Adventuresome(ness)
Alert(ness)
Assertive(ness)
Astute(ness)
Attention to details
Authentic(ity)
Authority, handles well
Aware(ness)
B
C
Calm(ness)
Candid(ness)
Challenges, thrives on
Character, has fine
Clothes, dresses well
Committed, commitment to growth
Competent (competence)
Concentration
Concerned
Conscientious(ness)
Cooperative (cooperation)
Courage(ous)
Creative, manifests creativity
Curious (curiosity)
D
Dependable (dependability)
Diplomatic (diplomacy)
Discreet
Driving (as, in ambition), drive
Dynamic(ness)
E
Easygoing(ness)
Emotional stability
Empathy (empathetic)
Enthusiastic (enthusiasm)
Exceptional
Experienced
Expert
Expressive(ness)
F
Firm(ness)
Flexible (flexibility)
G
Generous (generosity)
Gets along well with others
H
High energy level
Honest(y)
Humanly-oriented (warm)
I
Imaginative
Impulses, controls well
Initiating (initiative)
Innovative (innovation)
Insight(ful)
Integrity, displays constant
J
Judgment, has good
K
L

Loyal(ty)
M
Material world, deals well with the
N
Natural(ness)
O
Objective
Openminded(ness)
Optimistic (optimism)
Orderly (orderliness)
Outgoing(ness)
Outstanding
P
Patient (patience)
Penetrating
Perceptive(ness)
Persevering (perseverance)
Persisting (persistence)
Pioneering
Playful(ness)
Poise
Polite(ness)
Precise attainment of set goals,
    limits or standards
Punctual(ity)
Q
R
Reliable (reliability)
Resourceful(ness)
Responsible (responsibility)
Responsive(ness)
Risk-taking
S
Self-confident (confidence)
Self-control, good
Self-reliant (reliance)
Self-respect
Sense of humor, great
Sensitive (sensitivity)
Sincere (sincerity)
Sophisticated
Spontaneous (spontaneity)
Strikes balance, happy medium
Strong (as, under stress)
Successful
Sympathetic (sympathy), warm
T
Tactful(ness)
Takes nothing for granted
Thinks on his/her feet
Thorough(ness)
Tidy (tidiness)
Time, deals with well
    punctual (punctuality)
Tolerant (tolerance)
U
Uncommon
Unique
V
Versatile (versatility)
Vigor(ous)
W X Y Z

Use This List Twice: Underline. There are two ways to approach this list. First think of it as a list of *your own* possible Traits. *Underline* the ones which you think distinguish *You.*

And Then Circle. *Then* go back to the beginning, and this time approach the list as a list of People you would like to be surrounded by, at work. *Circle* the Traits that are most important to you, in the people you work with. If you desire different traits in your boss, from the traits you desire in your co-workers, or in those under you, make up three lists.

Compare. When you are done circling, do two things. First of all, compare *your* Traits with those you want to find in those around you at work. Are they the same? Don't be surprised if they are. Honest people usually like to be surrounded by honest people, and not by a bunch of liars. Etc. Etc.

And Prioritize. Secondly, of course, prioritize the list of stuff you want to have in those who surround you at work —unless you are going to be working alone, in which case, this is irrelevant. It may however have something to do with your clients or customers, so don't leap over this *too* quickly! Enter the results on page 53.

The Sixth Principle For Narrowing Down The Organizations,—Usually *After* You've Taken A Look At Them:

6 WHERE DO YOU WANT TO BE, GEOGRAPHICALLY SPEAKING?

It may be that you have no choice. Your mother lives nearby, at present, and she is on in years, and needs you to be near. And, you want to be near. So, geography may not look like a very important issue for you.

Mini-Geography. But, suppose you find as you go on, that there are two places which interest you. One is a 75-minute commute, and the other is a 10-minute commute. If you care about the length of your daily commute, then as you see, geography becomes a useful tool for deciding which one to go after. Mini-geography is operative here (one area or another, within your county or state). Maxi-geography might be operative at some other time of your life (whether to move from New York to California, or not).

Maxi-Geography. Indeed, it may be operative now, for you. To such an extent that you intend to go to the State of your choice, and there conduct your job-hunt, from the beginning. Or, to a lesser extent—such that, if two places come to your attention, and one is in your favorite City in the whole country (or world), while the other is not, the balance would be tipped for you in favor of the one which is in the City of your dreams.

Learn The Geography Lessons From Your Past. So, you need to think this out. If you want to move, need to move, but haven't the foggiest notion *Where,* try making a list of all the distasteful factors you have endured—geographically—since you were a small lad or lass. Conditions you hope you will never have to deal with again, as long as you live. Then turn those "negative" factors into "positives" again, prioritize them, and see what city or area it *sounds* like. Show the list to a number of your family or friends, if you have no clue.

Summarize It On The Tree Diagram. Whatever you come up with, mini-geography or maxi-, summarize it on the appropriate place, in the right side of the Tree diagram on page 53 — well, you surely know it by now.

Passive vs. Active Geography. Needless to say, you may be saving this Geography consideration just to help you weigh various attractive organizations, as you get down to the wire later on. On the other hand, Geography may be what's *driving* you, right now. If so, write the name of your "target" city or area, over near the "Goals of the Organization."

Well, there you have it. The six factors which will help you decide *WHERE* you want to use your skills. Now, on to the *HOW.*

Now that you just about have the "trunk" road completed, you have the necessary information in hand, to make some intelligent choices about which of these roads you are going to follow:

So, on to the third part of your homework:

How to identify the job you have just drawn a picture of, by name or by title;

How to identify the kind of organizations which have such a job;

How to get hired there.

There are three steps to the HOW part of your homework:

The First Step
On the Road To Your Job:
PRACTICE INTERVIEWING

You need to go out and practice talking to people. Just for practice. In a non-job, low-stress, practice interview situation—just for information. You can take someone with you, if you want. If you're shy, maybe you want to take someone with you who is more at ease with people than you are; and watch how he/she does it. Anyway, by yourself, or with someone:

Your task here is to go out and talk with somebody. Somebody at *A Place That Fascinates or Interests You*—like, say, an airport (how does it get run), a toy-store, a television station, or whatever; OR somebody who has *The Same Hobby or Leisure-Activity That You Do* —like, say, skiing, gardening, painting, music, color, or whatever; OR somebody who is working on *Some Issue*

That Fascinates or Interests You—like, say, affirmative action, or ecology, or assertiveness, or lower taxes, or whatever. Use your phone book (the Yellow Pages) or friends to find the kind of person you're looking for: e.g., for skiing, try a ski-supply store, or instructor.

When you find him or her, talk about your mutual enthusiasm. If you don't know what else to ask them, here are four suggestions: *1. How did you get into this work? Or: How did you get interested in this? 2. What do you like best about doing this? 3. What do you like least about doing this? 4. Where else could I find people who share this enthusiasm, or interest, or are interested in this issue?*

Then go visit the people they suggest, and ask them (if nothing else) the same four questions. Keep at this, practice it as long as you need to, until you feel comfortable talking to people.

Then, on to the next step.

The Second Step
On the Road To Your Job:
THOROUGH RESEARCHING
TO PUT IT ALL TOGETHER

Once you feel comfortable interviewing people, you are ready to go find what kind of job, and organizations, that THE TREE Diagram points to.

Look at the factors on the left-hand side of your diagram of THE TREE. Which factor is most important to you, in your next job or career? It will probably be something that is either on your "Special Knowledges" part of the diagram, or on your "Transferable Skills" part of the diagram. Put it down under #1, below. Which factor is next? Put it down under #2, below. And so on. This will give you *the order* in which to do your research.

If you don't know what kinds of organizations to approach, read, mark, learn and inwardly digest chapters six and seven in *What Color Is Your Parachute?* There you will find lots of pointers and clues.

You should show your list of favorite transferable skills to your friends and family, and ask them to tell you what jobs come to mind as they read over the list. *Then,* and only then, also show them your list of top five Favorite Special Knowledges, and ask them what jobs now come to mind, that you might find worth exploring.

RESEARCHING YOUR IDEAL JOB

In the first stage of my research I'm going to identify someone whose job uses/ is characterized by

1. _____

In the second stage of my research I'm going to identify someone whose job uses/ is characterized by

1. _____ AND

2. _____

In the third stage of my research I'm going to identify someone whose job uses/ is characterized by

1. _____ AND

2. _____ AND

3. _____

In the fourth stage of my research I'm going to identify someone whose job uses/ is characterized by

1. _____ AND

2. _____ AND

3. _____ AND

4. _____

In the fifth stage of my research I'm going to...
(You can surely finish this diagram for yourself, on a separate sheet of blank paper.)

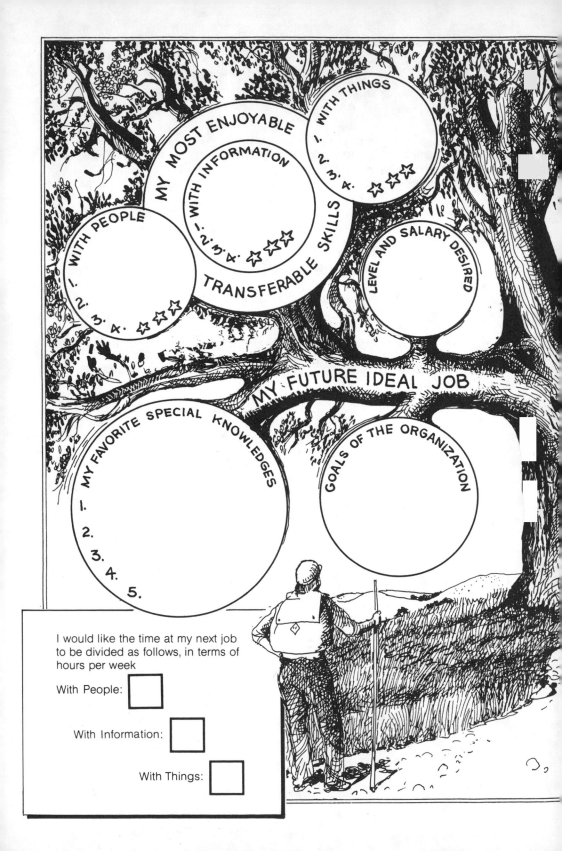

MY MOST ENJOYABLE TRANSFERABLE SKILLS

WITH THINGS
1.
2.
3.
4.

WITH INFORMATION
1.
2.
3.
4.

WITH PEOPLE
1.
2.
3.
4.

LEVEL AND SALARY DESIRED

MY FUTURE IDEAL JOB

MY FAVORITE SPECIAL KNOWLEDGES
1.
2.
3.
4.
5.

GOALS OF THE ORGANIZATION

I would like the time at my next job to be divided as follows, in terms of hours per week

With People: ☐

With Information: ☐

With Things: ☐

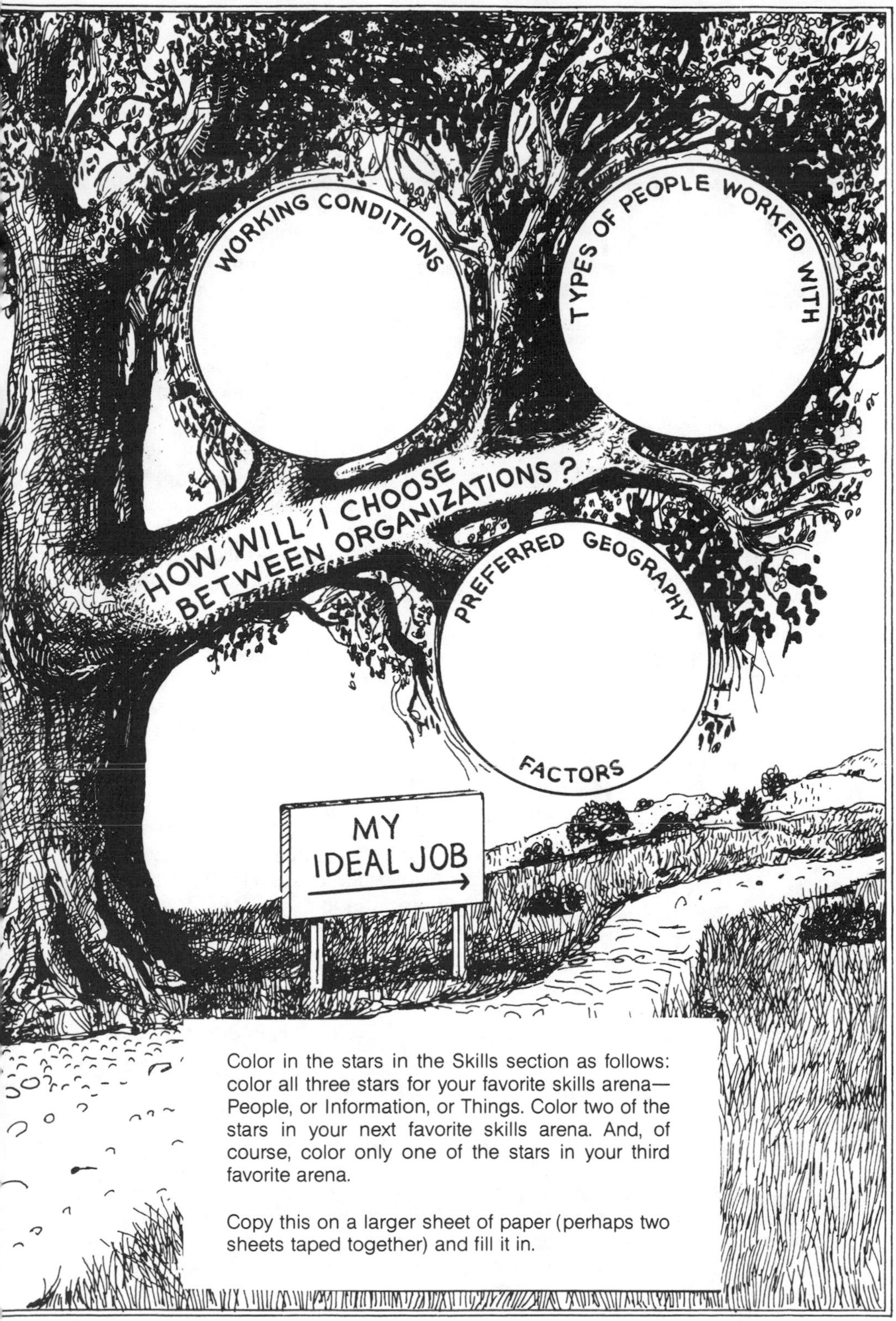

WORKING CONDITIONS

TYPES OF PEOPLE WORKED WITH

HOW WILL I CHOOSE BETWEEN ORGANIZATIONS?

PREFERRED GEOGRAPHY

FACTORS

MY IDEAL JOB

Color in the stars in the Skills section as follows: color all three stars for your favorite skills arena— People, or Information, or Things. Color two of the stars in your next favorite skills arena. And, of course, color only one of the stars in your third favorite arena.

Copy this on a larger sheet of paper (perhaps two sheets taped together) and fill it in.

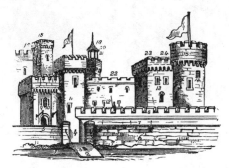

If at any time during this research, you can't identify someone who actually holds the job you are interested in holding, ask your contacts for help.

Whenever you run into a stone wall, use your contacts (friends, family, school alumni, former employers, etc.) for suggestions as to where you can turn next.

The Third And Last Step On The Road To Your Job: GO VISIT

In the course of the above research, you will not only discover the kind of job(s) you would most like to have, but you will—in the course of your research —inevitably discover what organizations have such jobs.

Now, your task is GO VISIT THE TWO OR THREE ORGANIZATIONS YOU LIKED THE BEST and tell them so— together with why (your chance to discuss all the factors on The Tree Picture of the job you are looking for).

Whether they have a vacancy or not, is immaterial. You are going to seek out in each organization among your top three or so, the person who has the power to hire (not the personnel department); and you are going to tell him or her

a) what impressed you about their organization, during your research,

b) what sorts of challenges, needs or "problems" (go slow in using this latter word with sensitive employers) your

survey suggested exists in this field in general, and with this place in particular —that intrigue you.

c) what skills seem to you to be needed, in order to meet those challenges or needs in his or her organization.

d) that fact that you have these skills (here use the information summarized on the Tree Diagram).*

They, for their part, will have four basic questions they will want to know the answers to, about YOU:

a) why are you here (i.e., why did you pick out their organization)?

b) what can you do for them (i.e., what are your skills and special knowledges)?

c) what kind of person are you (i.e., what are your goals/values, self-management, etc.)?

d) how much are you going to cost them (your salary *range*—maximum, minimum)?

They may ask you directly about these, or they may try to find them out by just letting the interview happen.

Hopefully, this will lead to your being offered the job. If it does not, go on to the next place you liked the best.

For further information about any part of the above process, reread chapters 5-7 in Parachute.

Good luck, Peace, and Shalom.

*Some Final Homework Before The Job Interview

You will interpret your skills better, if you first have done a little exercise on yourself. You can only do this exercise, when you have a very particular place in mind as your "target" organization— where you *most* want to get hired. The exercise, then, goes like this:

● Make up a grid that looks like this:

● And fill it in (Example:)

I I	II One of your verbs	III What? To what? To whom?	IV Problem you are going to solve	V Similarity of that company to new 'target'	VI Results: tangible facts and figures
I	researched	the subject of memory	in order to help people in my company see the value of memory training	in a company which like yours, had less than 50 employees	and showed my boss that memory train-ing would increase retention of training 400% — The Co. instituted the training + it was very successful
I					
I					
I					
I					
I					
I					

● and then take the following steps (next page):

Go back to the Tree diagram, and look at the skills you have listed there, under "Skills with People," "Skills with Information," and "Skills with Things." Enter them under "column II." Put them in the past tense, e.g., "organizing" becomes "organized." Thus far this grid will then read: "I organized..."

Fleshing Out The Skill. Now what you want to do at this time, is think of whatever achievement you have done, which demonstrated that you indeed have this skill. It *may be* that you will want to use one of your seven stories. On the other hand, you may think of a much more impressive achievement, now, which demonstrated that you had this skill. In the rest of this grid, you are going to describe it, under a certain form.

Filling Out The Form. In column III you say what it is you organized (or whatever the verb was)—it will always be some kind of People, or some kind of Information/Data, or some kind of Thing. In column IV you say what problem you were trying to solve.

The Bridge Between Where You Were And Where You Want To Go. In column V you say what similarities there were and are between the organization or place where you did this thing, and the organization you are now approaching for a job. This is the part of this grid that you will have to give the most thought to. What *is* it that this organization, and the place where you did this

achievement, *have in common?* Think hard. What you are trying to get across is that you know the problems of *this* organization before you, because you dealt with something similar in the past.

For example: "...in an organization which, like yours, had less than 20 employees..." OR: "I did this in an organization, which, like yours, is seeking to be the leader in its field." Etc.

Results That Can Be Seen, Or—Better—Measured. In column VI, put down the results of your action. Because you did "so and so," trying to solve "such and such" a problem, you were successful, and this is how we know it: "blah, blah."

Do The Same With Your Other Favorite Skills. Fill in the rest of the grid in the same manner, always listing your *next most favorite skill* each time you proceed on to the next line.

Oral Or Written. You should keep the results of this exercise at your fingertips or—better—at the forefront of your mind, when you go on the interview. You will then be able to truly demonstrate that you have the skills you claim to have.

If You Want Additional Help

Bernard Haldane Associates' Job and Career Building, by Richard Germann and Peter Arnold. 1981, 1980. Ten Speed Press, Box 7123, Berkeley, CA 94707. $6.95 + $.75 postage and handling.

Who's Hiring Who? by Richard C. Lathrop. 1977. At your local bookstore, or order directly from Ten Speed Press, Box 7123, Berkeley, CA 94707. $7.95 + $.75 postage and handling.

Making Vocational Choices: A Theory of Careers, by John L. Holland. 1973. Order directly from Prentice-Hall, Inc., Englewood Cliffs, NJ 07632. $15.95, paperback.

Where Do I Go From Here With My Life? by John C. Crystal and Richard N. Bolles. 1974. Ten Speed Press, Box 7123, Berkeley, CA 94707. $9.95 + $.75 postage and handling.

Job Power Now! The Young People's Job Finding Guide, by Bernard Haldane, Jean Haldane and Lowell Martin. 1976. At your local bookstore or order directly from Acropolis Books Ltd., 2400 17th St. N.W., Washington, DC 20009. $4.95, paperback.

Acknowledgements

I would like to acknowledge my debt, in this Map, to all the fine original thinkers in this field, who gave me many ideas for better helping job-hunters or career-changers:

to Sidney Fine, for thinking out the whole concept of People, Data, and Things, originally for the research on the Dictionary of Occupational Titles; I have done a kind of "rhapsody" on his work, but without his work there would be none of mine;

to John Crystal, for so very much—he was my original mentor in this field; we are particularly indebted to him in this Map for the fundamental distinction between WHAT, WHERE and HOW, as well as the concept of the Practice Field Survey;

to Daniel Porot, for so many ideas I have used particularly in this new revised version of the Map—most particularly the concepts of "job beggar," "art vs. technique," "the handicaps of the job-hunter," and "the final homework";

to John Holland, for the concepts at the base of the Party Exercise, and his whole system of RIASEC;

to Bernard Haldane, for the basic concept of doing detailed skill identification based upon past achievements.

All of us who find this Map a helpful guide are, in the end, indebted to these pioneers. And I for my part not only gratefully acknowledge their ideas, but also my gratitude for their friendship.

Those entering the job-market for the first time, and desiring a simpler skill-list than we have provided here, are referred to *The Three Boxes of Life,* in which the Beginning Version of the Quick Job-Hunting Map may be found. Or that version may be ordered separately, by writing directly to Ten Speed Press, P.O. Box 7123, Berkeley, CA 94707. $1.25 + $.50 for postage and handling.

Notes

Notes

May we introduce other
Ten Speed Press books you may find useful . . .
over three million people have already.

What Color Is Your Parachute? by Richard N. Bolles
The Three Boxes of Life by Richard N. Bolles
Who's Hiring Who by Richard Lathrop
Bernard Haldane Associates' Job & Career Building
by Richard Germann and Peter Arnold
Finding a Job by Nathan H. Azrin, Ph.D., and Victoria Besalel
Finding Facts Fast by Alden Todd
Mail Order Moonlighting by Cecil Hoge
Bear's Guide to Non-Traditional College Degrees
by John Bear, Ph.D.
Computer Wimp by John Bear, Ph.D.
The Moosewood Cookbook by Mollie Katzen
The Enchanted Broccoli Forest by Mollie Katzen
Sailing the Farm by Ken Neumeyer
Write Right! by Jan Venolia
The Wellness Workbook
by Regina Sara Ryan and John W. Travis, M.D.
How to Grow More Vegetables by John Jeavons
Anybody's Bike Book by Tom Cuthbertson
Pleasure Packing by Robert S. Wood
Sweaty Palms by H. Anthony Medley
Finding Money For College by John Bear, Ph.D.

You will find them in your bookstore or library,
or you can send for our *free* catalog:

Ten Speed Press
P O Box 7123
Berkeley, California 94707